The Beginning...

Laine Renee

BookLeaf Publishing

Presentation by *BookLeaf Publishing*

Web: www.bookleafpub.com

E-mail: info@bookleafpub.com

ISBN: 978-93-95890-00-7

First edition 2022

To the confusion that gave me the gift of writing.

Writer's Block for Today

I write every day.
Today,
Is a box.
I've been banging against the walls,
The walls expel music each time I bang.
Not beautiful music,
The music that makes your heart beat a little faster when you reach out in the dark.
It's a sound of crushing fear.

I tempt myself into believing the box around me doesn't exist.
And its crushing weight is just a memory.
Because I know I would never be able to handle the realities of today.
The harsh truths that I,
I am not able to come up with the words.
I am not able to paint a picture for others.
I am not able to dive deeper into my mind and anchor onto something that truly will hold me down.

The box travels with me.
For today it carries me.
That fear holds me.
So tight that it does not matter if I like it or not.

So after a while, I stop banging on the walls.
I let myself sink into a curled-up ball,
And waste the time away.
Then when it finally starts to break down by itself,
And the fear-inspiring music fades into the distance of my mind,
A slow classical piano piece starts to play.
And as the piano sings
My mind starts to unravel.
The words of bright colors and sentences like brush strokes come back to me in a raging sense of peace.
After floating through an empty head,
The colors get turned into a painting,
The brush strokes find their home.
The box lets down its defenses,
And I,
I get to write again.

Untitled

When everything, all distant and close,
Evaporates from that drawer you keep inside of your heart,
And your head turns to the ground,
As your eyes let open the ocean held inside,
You water the earth around you.
The dried, shriveled-up grass around your feet starts smelling sweet,
The perfume of growth surrounding your feet.
Flowers start blooming,
Wrapping around your ankles,
Their petals open their faces to the sky to say thank you.
The sapling your tears soaked into grew close to you and the garden at your feet.
It grew vines, twisting their way all the way up your legs.

As your eyes start to become clear of their salty ocean streams,
You catch a glimpse of melting colors.
Though the tears have left your eyes with distorting lenses,
Your arms reach to wipe away the blur,
But they are stuck between vines and leaves,

Your body caught in a net of growth your eyes
themselves have grown with their rivers seeming
never-ending,
Only to start again at the thought of how cruel a
moment like this must be.

A little less time

There isn't a goodbye for us to share,
Only the bitterness of the bitter-sweet moment itself.
A short see you later.
I love you, my friend.
You will tower over seas and mountains.
Your beauty and grace will grow even more than they have already blossomed.
Your love will withstand storms of any kind.
This short sad goodbye will not be forever.
Soon enough days will come together where we dance again.
But while we are all apart,
Don't let your light stop but continue to shine through the pain of leaving.
New challenges,
New people,
New experiences,
All waiting for you!
You, my friend.
You are incredible.
I love you.
See you later.

A response to another poets work...

I want to be chosen.
To have my soul leap from my being into words that speak to the very grass that sways between my toes,
To have the airflow into my lungs with a burning fire sensation.

I want to be free.
To be free through all the things my mind is pacing through,
To be freed by spilling the ink over the pages of thousands of journals to create music in sentences.
I want to live in through my pen.
to be the ink that is spilling out of it, flowing in time with such perfect rhythm, telling the stories my mouth refuses to let out.
I want to suffocate no longer,
under the pressure, under the ideas, under the anxiety, I want to tear from the hands of my fears gripping my neck so tightly making it unable for me to exist any longer.
I want to sing to people.

to have passion beyond what this world could
ever know.
I want to give myself.
I want to lose myself.
I want to bend and be crushed by the romantic
tumbleweeds of life

Untitled

There is a beauty I can't reach.
It's in the moments when the wind starts to blow
and my heart beats a little faster.
In the branches of the dead trees when they
crackle with noise.
It's floating with their leaves flying down to the
earth on their fateful last journey.
It's in the ground as it readies itself to accept
every living thing to find its home on it.
There is a beauty I will never understand.
It's worlds away from this world I dream in.
It's behind everything, every moment of
tranquility, every accidental touch from a
not-so-distant stranger.
It lives in worlds behind those hushed relaxed
movements the earth makes without being
noticed.
Oh to be so empty-headed that you enter those
worlds so freely and transform into the beauty
we see, no longer blind to all the glories of
living in a broken forsaken world.
Maybe then the beauty would not be as unique.
Maybe it's the other hidden world that makes
this world so individual.

I don't think my heart can truly be able to handle
the undying strange poetic beauty everything has
in this world.
Is it a gift or a curse to be able to feel so intense
at every moment?

Untitled

I create in my head,
Poems I can't find the words for,
For I create them in color and sounds
I get trapped inside of them
Placing them in different positions like an artist using their thumb to find the center of their painting
I can never seem to find the perfect placement for them
So I exist in never-ending colorful poems floating in my head
A chaotic beauty overflowing all senses
But I must keep creating,
To stay alive.

Seventeen

welcome,
the door just opened
the flowers just lifted their heads,
the sun moved from behind that dark cloud
a song created by all the music heard is playing,
so powerful it gives the heart an ache
the earth welcomes you
the skies praise above
your face is forced to turn above
for the glories and grace is above
God welcomes you
Sixteen was a slow tide change,
a feeling of forever swept sixteen along
seventeen will be quick and hurried,
but a good hurried
growth will be a healthy green
dancing will be normal,
so welcome,
come through the door.

To be a part of nature

I want to dissolve into nature,
To have the moist grass growing into my skin
and surround my senses.
I want to feel the clouds moving and the roaring
thunder rumbling my bones...

Today

Today feels like fresh sheets and a cry in the sun.
Today feels like a warm bath after swimming in
cold water for hours.
Today feels like a flower bloomed across the
sky.
Today feels like music blasting out of the car
that you pass with people screaming the lyrics.
Today feels like the city and the country are two
very good friends.
Today feels like eating raspberries straight after
picking.
Today feels like wavy hair on the beach.
Today feels like the sound of a creek running
down rocks.
Today feels like peace and love.
Today feels like home.

Letting Go

Walking through the rooms for this last time, it's
opening doors to memories I had forgotten
The memories are hard to see in my head
They pierce my heart and create a longing for
them again,
Make me regret ever growing up
I don't want to let go yet.
I'm afraid if I don't let go I won't get any
closure
Nothing to officially close the past dozen
chapters of my story
it's the time for a new adventure,
But saying goodbye to my past is the hardest
thing I have had to do
My childhood.
The pure moments i had in life,
Pure imagination being wiped from my
existence.
Does growing up have to be this painful lord?

The Clock

Time likes to mock me.
The clock sits on the counter,
Staring me down as each second passes and as I move about.
Every time I feel the urge to look, I regret it.
Only a couple of minutes, a couple of seconds,
not enough time has passed in that moment
yet for the other moments,
the most beautiful of moments,
time likes to play tricks on us and speed up.

The clock yells at me and says I haven't done much.
I haven't done enough.
The clock yells at me and says I need to be better.
I am not good enough.
The time flies while it sits still.
Every moment ceases to exist as soon as it has come.
Everything has to fade into memory.
No longer reality.
But yet it feels so slow.
Everything coming and going so quickly, a time-lapse and slow motion.

A Feeling

Am I designed to always reach out,
Towards a feeling?
Towards a piece of myself?
That will never be close enough to become a part of me,
Will I always be cursed with the burden of longing?
Why does my soul ache with a terrible fear of never looking beyond?
The invisible wall between me and that beauty I can not touch.
The beauty I constantly run towards in my mind,
And the beauty that is hidden so far behind things it is so invisible to the everyday person.
Or it screams at you.
Like it does to me.
I reach out towards it trying to grasp upon such beauty.
It's so much deeper in me.
The beauty places a hope inside of me that makes me long for it to be a piece of me.

The Glass and the Boy

He is in love,
He is looking at the glass that's glittering so warm and heavenly with colors.
He sees movements in the glass that no one else can.
He is creating ideas and dancing in his imagination through memories he wants to design with the glass.
He looks INTO the glass, not at it.
He holds the warmth and colors with shining eyes that show the depths of the ocean.
He loves it, he wants to protect the glass with his entire being.
He loves the glass,
Even though it's been cracked and peices that have been broken are glued in trying to repair it.
He loves the glass, for the glass glitters warm and heavenly with colors.

I love you

being told I love you,
the feeling never goes away.
you know when the ice melts and spring turns into summer,
that's what being told I love you is supposed to feel like.

being told I love you,
the feeling I have will never sit well.
you know I can't help but cry every night even if you remind me of your love.
that's how I live in my fears and in content,
that's not how being told I love you is supposed to feel.
being told I love you is a different sort of emotion,
none that has been given a word to describe the overwhelming anxiety I have because of it,
you know me not as well as you need to and not as quick as a stranger.
maybe that's what hurts is you telling me you love me and you don't even know one secret I have.

being told I love you.
It’s supposed to happen later,
the feelings can't happen when they are not
there.
you know when the ice forgets to melt and
spring doesn't come?
that’s what I feel in my heart for those quiet
words we speak,
being told I love you,
I love you will never love me the way I despise
it.

Untitled

Again, I cried last night.
If one more shaking tear takes its grave upon my pillow,
My heart will begin to peel from my chest in search of your love.
In search of your love, I will lose who I have become.
So I must hold in my tears,
Wipe my eyes,
Hold my hands against my chest to keep my heart from falling out and running away,
And carry on with a still ache in my body.

I wanted you more

I wanted you more than the moon
more than the night
that so softly held me in the darkness.
more than the dreams that I hide behind.
I wanted you more
more than the quiet.
and more than my tears.
and maybe that sounds selfish
selfish for me.
more than the warmth
of my own damn bed.
I'd put my thumb out on the side of the road if I
could just have you for one day.
I wanted you more.
more than the times
I wish I could run.
run far far away
from all of my fears
and all of my lies
and all the weight that pushes me down
I wanted you more than my escape
I wanted you more
more than the shadows
more than the stars
more than the poems

more than the peace,
that I’ll wake up okay.

Quiet

People are angered by quiet souls.
They wish those quiet souls could be crushed by
the weight of life.
They try to make the quiet souls uncomfortable
to the point of becoming enraged.
They are uncomfortable with the peace that
resounds from the quiet souls.
It's hard to understand that a quiet soul is the
strongest of souls,
The unsettling peace it gives off is the darkness
of the mind,
Hidden away in the depths.
Quiet souls are passionate souls.
The beautiful souls who see true beauty.

Untitled

I fall in love so easily.
I figured out the simple formula to it all.
the simple looks, and touches in the mind, then
the feeling that you need them.
it all comes too easily for me.
it weighs my heart down to know that I have
created a jungle gym of trap doors for it to fall
down into.
I started to think a person is the right one.
someone I could grow with and into loving.
but there are always complications to it.
age, distance, and life situations.
something is always in the way.
So why must I continue to fall in love so easily?

Lonely timing

The wind moves so softly when you close your
eyes.
The water's ripples and the grass's welcoming
dance.
The smell of the season slipping into the air
waking the soul.

It's the beauty underneath.
It's the worlds beyond.
It's the peace you must set yourself free in.

The sky above the earth below, and the gliding
clouds forming pictures, moving, motioning.

The tree's soft rustle,
The simple symphony of the birds.

It's the time, the way it stops.
It's the oxygen, the way it begs for you to
breathe.
It's the nothing in it all.

It's the loneliness in the timing.

Little Girl, Lost and Forgotten

the ways of a little girl.
careless and free
running through fields of amber and gold.
careless and free
imagination running wild
careless and free
dancing in the winter sun
seeing the cold as beauty for it has its time just
as the summer,
careless and free
floating in canoes of daydreams
careless and free
hair messy and wild
careless and free
laughing without covering your mouth yet shy
and quiet
careless and free
writing stories, oh the many stories
careless and free
creating worlds away from home
careless and free
loving everyone and anyone
sharing grace beyond your touch
careless and free

light and dark simultaneously
sinful and angel
careless and free
longing for adventure and wide-eyed
careless and free
fun-filled and creativeness, stretching arms
through the woods you grew up in
careless and free
daring and silly, a beast
careless and free
daddy's little girl.
careless and free
German blood pulsing in your American body
careless and free
always willing to disrupt life
careless and free
a wild child.
careless and free
young girl longing for years,
longing for lighter years.
careless and free
not knowing the consequences
careless and free
a child's smile slowly turns to a grimace
careless and free
to ready to change
careless and free
please stay in the present for as long as you can.
careless and free

it’s too late.
worried and trapped
little girl grew up.
murdered by her own older self.
lost. and forgotten.

Untitled

I am the space between the lines you write.
I am the breath between the breeze,
I am the darkness between your eyes,
I am the light shining through your words.
Who am I?

www.ingramcontent.com/pod-product-compliance
Lightning Source LLC
Chambersburg PA
CBHW051755130826
49812CB00033B/1162
9789395890007